BRITISH RAILWAYS STEAMING ON THE SOUTH COAST

Compiled by
PETER HAY

DEFIANT PUBLICATIONS
190 Yoxall Road,
Shirley, Solihull,
West Midlands

Printed on behalf of Richard Netherwood Ltd by Gorenjski Tisk, Yugolslavıa

CURRENT STEAM PHOTOGRAPH ALBUMS AVAILABLE
FROM DEFIANT PUBLICATIONS

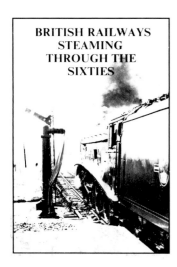

BRITISH RAILWAYS STEAMING THROUGH THE SIXTIES

VOLUME 11
A4 size - Hardback. 100 pages
-180 b/w photographs.
£10.95 + £1.00 postage.
ISBN 0 946857 24 5.

BRITISH RAILWAYS STEAMING THROUGH THE SIXTIES

VOLUME 12
A4 size - Hardback. 100 pages
-182 b/w photographs.
£11.95 + £1.00 postage.
ISBN 0 946857 27 X.

BRITISH RAILWAYS STEAMING THROUGH THE SIXTIES

VOLUME 13
A4 size - Hardback. 100 pages
-182 b/w photographs.
£11.95 + £1.00 postage.
ISBN 0 946857 33 4.

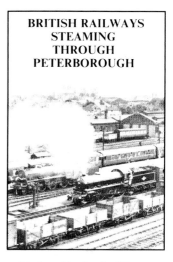

BRITISH RAILWAYS STEAMING THROUGH PETERBOROUGH

A4 size - Hardback. 100 pages
-163 b/w photographs.
£10.95 + £1.00 postage.
ISBN 0 946857 26 1.

BRITISH RAILWAYS STEAMING ON THE WESTERN REGION

VOLUME 3
A4 size - Hardback. 100 pages
-179 b/w photographs.
£10.95 + £1.00 postage.
ISBN 0 946857 25 3.

BRITISH RAILWAYS STEAMING ON THE WESTERN REGION

IN PREPARATION

VOLUME 4

BRITISH RAILWAYS STEAMING ON THE SOUTH COAST

A4 size - Hardback. 100 pages
-182 b/w photographs.
£11.95 + £1.00 postage.
ISBN 0 946857 29 6.

BRITISH RAILWAYS STEAMING ON THE SOUTHERN REGION

IN PREPARATION

VOLUME 3

BRITISH RAILWAYS STEAMING ON THE LONDON MIDLAND REGION

VOLUME 3
A4 size - Hardback. 100 pages
-181 b/w photographs.
£11.95 + £1.00 postage.
ISBN 0 946857 28 8.

BRITISH RAILWAYS STEAMING ON THE LONDON MIDLAND REGION

IN PREPARATION

VOLUME 4

BRITISH RAILWAYS STEAMING ON THE EX-LNER LINES

A4 siz
-187 b/
£11.95
ISBN 0

BRITISH RAILWAYS STEAMING ON THE SCOTTISH REGION

IN PREPARATION

VOLUME 1

CURRENT STEAM PHOTOGRAPH ALBUMS AVAILABLE
FROM DEFIANT PUBLICATIONS

VOLUME 1
A4 size - Hardback. 100 pages
-180 b/w photographs.
£8.95 + £1.00 postage.
ISBN 0 946857 12 1.

VOLUME 2
A4 size - Hardback. 100 pages
-180 b/w photographs.
£8.95 + £1.00 postage.
ISBN 0 946857 13 X.

VOLUME 3
A4 size - Hardback. 100 pages
-180 b/w photographs.
£9.95 + £1.00 postage.
ISBN 0 946857 16 4.

VOLUME 4
A4 size - Hardback. 100 pages
-180 b/w photographs.
£9.95 + £1.00 postage.
ISBN 0 946857 17 2.

VOLUME 5
A4 size - Hardback. 100 pages
-180 b/w photographs.
£9.95 + £1.00 postage.
ISBN 0 946857 22 9.

VOLUME 6
A4 size - Hardback. 100 pages
-180 b/w photographs.
£9.95 + £1.00 postage.
ISBN 0 946857 23 7.

VOLUME 7
A4 size - Hardback. 100 pages
-180 b/w photographs.
£11.95 + £1.00 postage.
ISBN 0 946857 31 8.

VOLUME 8
A4 size - Hardback. 100 pages
-180 b/w photographs.
£11.95 + £1.00 postage.
ISBN 0 946857 32 6.

BRITISH RAILWAYS
STEAMING
THROUGH THE
FIFTIES

IN
PREPARATION

BRITISH RAILWAYS
STEAMING
THROUGH THE
FIFTIES

IN
PREPARATION

BRITISH RAILWAYS
STEAMING
THROUGH CREWE,
DONCASTER,
EASTLEIGH AND
SWINDON

IN
PREPARATION

BRITISH RAILWAYS
STEAMING
FROM ST. PANCRAS
TO ST. ENOCH

IN
PREPARATION

VOLUME 9

OTHER TITLES AVAILABLE FROM DEFIANT PUBLICATIONS

PRICES VARY FROM £1 to £3.80 INCLUDING POSTAGE

WHAT HAPPENED TO STEAM

Volume One

THE GREAT WESTERN

2800 Class 2-8-0's
&
R O D Class 2-8-0's

WHAT HAPPENED TO STEAM

This series of booklets, 50 in all, is designed to inform the reader of the allocations, re-allocations and dates of withdrawal of steam locomotives during their last years of service. From 1957 onwards and finally where the locomotives concerned were stored and subsequently scrapped.

BR STEAM SHED ALLOCATIONS

This series lists all individual steam locomotives based at the different parent depots of B.R. from January 1957 until each depot either closed to steam or closed completely. An attractive book binder is available for this thirteen book series.

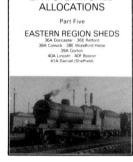

B.R. STEAM SHED ALLOCATIONS

Part One

WESTERN REGION SHEDS

81A Old Oak Common · 81F Oxford
82A Bristol (Bath Road) · 82F Weymouth
83A Newton Abbot · 83G Penzance

WHAT HAPPENED TO STEAM

THE
L.N.E.R.
B1 4-6-0's

WHAT HAPPENED TO STEAM

THE SOUTHERN
H15, N15, 'KING ARTHURS' S15
& 'LORD NELSON' 4-6-0's.
G16 4-8-0 TANKS.
H16 4-6-2 TANKS.

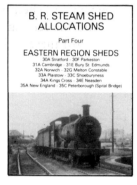

B. R. STEAM SHED ALLOCATIONS

Part Four

EASTERN REGION SHEDS

30A Stratford · 30F Parkeston
31A Cambridge · 31E Bury St. Edmunds
32A Norwich · 32G Melton Constable
33A Plaistow · 33C Shoeburyness
34A Kings Cross · 34E Neasden
35A New England · 35C Peterborough (Spital Bridge)

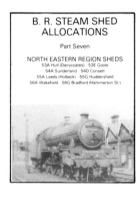

B. R. STEAM SHED ALLOCATIONS

Part Five

EASTERN REGION SHEDS

36A Doncaster · 36E Retford
38A Colwick · 38E Woodford Halse
39A Gorton
40A Lincoln · 40F Boston
41A Darnall (Sheffield)

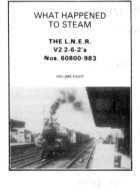

WHAT HAPPENED TO STEAM

THE LNW 0-8-0's
Nos. 48895-49674
L & Y TANK CLASSES -
Nos. 50636-51546
&
L & Y 0-6-0's Nos. 52089-52529

Volume Forty-Seven

WHAT HAPPENED TO STEAM

THE
LONDON MIDLAND
2F & 3F
0-6-0 TANKS
Nos. 47160-9 & 47200-681

VOLUME FORTY-FIVE

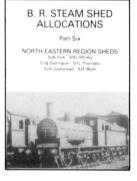

B. R. STEAM SHED ALLOCATIONS

Part Six

NORTH EASTERN REGION SHEDS

50A York · 50G Whitby
51A Darlington · 51L Thornaby
52A Gateshead · 52F Blyth

B. R. STEAM SHED ALLOCATIONS

Part Seven

NORTH EASTERN REGION SHEDS

53A Hull (Dairycoates) · 53E Goole
54A Sunderland · 54D Consett
55A Leeds (Holbeck) · 55G Huddersfield
56A Wakefield · 56G Bradford (Hammerton St.)

WHAT HAPPENED TO STEAM

THE L.N.E.R.
V2 2-6-2's
Nos. 60800-983

VOLUME EIGHT

WHAT HAPPENED TO STEAM

THE B.R.

CLASS 4 4-6-0's & 2-6-0's
Nos. 75000-79 & 76000-114

B. R. STEAM SHED ALLOCATIONS

Part Eight

SCOTTISH REGION SHEDS

60A Inverness · 60E Forres
61A Kittybrewster · 61C Keith
62A Thornton Junction · 62C Dunfermline
63A Perth · 63D Oban
64A St. Margarets (Edinburgh) · 64G Hawick
65A Eastfield (Glasgow) · 65J Fort William
66A Polmadie (Glasgow) · 66D Greenock (Ladyburn)
67A Corkerhill (Glasgow) · 67D Ardrossan
68A Carlisle (Kingmoor) · 68E Carlisle (Canal)
St. Rollox Works

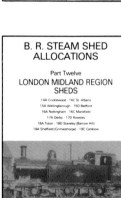

B. R. STEAM SHED ALLOCATIONS

Part Nine

SOUTHERN REGION SHEDS

70A Nine Elms · 70H Ryde (I.O.W.)
71A Eastleigh · 71J Highbridge
72A Exmouth Jct. · 72F Wadebridge
73A Stewarts Lane · 73E Faversham
74A Ashford · 74E St. Leonards
75A Brighton · 75F Tunbridge Wells

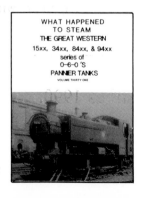

WHAT HAPPENED TO STEAM

Volume Twenty Eight

THE
L.M.S.
8F 2-8-0's
&
Somerset and Dorset
7F 2-8-0's

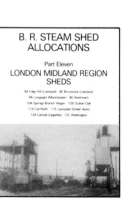

WHAT HAPPENED TO STEAM
THE GREAT WESTERN

15xx, 34xx, 84xx, & 94xx
series of
0-6-0's
PANNIER TANKS

VOLUME THIRTY ONE

B. R. STEAM SHED ALLOCATIONS

Part Eleven

LONDON MIDLAND REGION SHEDS

8A Edge Hill (Liverpool) · 8E Brunswick (Liverpool)
9A Longsight (Manchester) · 9G Northwich
10A Springs Branch Wigan · 10D Sutton Oak
11A Carnforth · 11E Lancaster (Green Ayre)
12A Carlisle (Upperby) · 12C Workington

B. R. STEAM SHED ALLOCATIONS

Part Twelve

LONDON MIDLAND REGION SHEDS

14A Cricklewood · 14C St. Albans
15A Wellingborough · 15D Bedford
16A Nottingham · 16C Mansfield
17A Derby · 17D Rowsley
18A Toton · 18D Staveley (Barrow Hill)
19A Sheffield (Grimesthorpe) · 19C Canklow

ACKNOWLEDGEMENTS

Grateful thanks are extended to the following contributors of photographs not only for their use in this book but for their kind patience and long term loan of negatives/photographs whilst this book was being compiled.

C. H. ATTWELL
CHICHESTER

A. E. BENNETT
ACLE

H. H. BLEADS
BIRMINGHAM

B. W. L. BROOKSBANK
LONDON

N. L. BROWNE
ALDERSHOT

A. N. H. GLOVER
BIRMINGHAM

PETER HAY
HOVE

J. HEAD
EASTBOURNE

A. C. INGRAM
WISBECH

ALAN JONES
BATH

D. K. JONES
MOUNTAIN ASH

J. H. W. KENT
BRIGHTON

H. M. MADGWICK
WORTHING

N. E. PREEDY
HUCCLECOTE

G. W. SHARPE
BARNSLEY

N. W. SPRINKS
DINAS POWIS

A. SWAIN
WEMBLEY

Front Cover — In pristine condition, complete with headboard and chocolate and cream coaches, a gleaming GWR *Castle* Class 4-6-0 No 5052 *Earl of Radnor* departs from Dawlish station in a flurry of steam and heads towards Paddington and its home base of 81A Old Oak Common, with the up *Torbay Express* on 29th August 1958. (A.N.H. Glover)

ISBN 0 946857 29 6

(c) PETER HAY & DEFIANT PUBLICATIONS 1991
FIRST PUBLISHED 1991

INTRODUCTION

BRITISH RAILWAYS STEAMING ON THE SOUTH COAST is a companion volume to that covering the EAST COAST MAIN LINE which appeared in 1986. As well as the native GWR and SR engines, BR Standard and a few LMS designs put in an appearance as a consequence of nationalisation, long distance excursions and the much lamented Somerset & Dorset Joint Line.

Many of the trains pictured were carrying holidaymakers, for in the 1950's the age of the charter flight to the Costas of Europe had not yet arrived and the seaside resorts of the south coast welcomed thousands of families in the weeks of high summer, most of them coming by train.

Many of the smaller resorts of Devon and Cornwall were served by spurs from the main lines, by branch trains of great charm, luring many boys on holiday away from the beach to sample the delights of the station. Here, far from the eye of authority, there was often the chance of being invited onto the footplate and even — always to be remembered — taken for a ride on the engine as it did some shunting.

Because the south coast has little, if any, heavy industry, there are far more pictures of passenger than freight trains within the pages of this album, though in the fifties the majority of stations, large and small, still had operational goods yards. These had once catered for a two-way business but by the time of these pictures, most of the traffic consisted of coal for the local fireplaces. Agricultural products and most other commodities travelled by road, though coal remained faithful to rail. But in the last decade before near universal car ownership, the holidaymakers came by train.

BRITISH RAILWAYS STEAMING ON THE SOUTH COAST is divided into six county sections, from east to west. Dorset is the only county where there has never been a railway route either along the coast, or parallel to it a short distance inland. Right along the Channel coast I have tried to confine the pictorial coverage to lines and stations no more than ten miles inland, although you may find a few exceptions. No attempt has been made to offer a picture at every station along the coastal strip. Rather, you have the result of individuals' choices, to photograph where and what they thought interesting at the time.

The captions, for better or worse, are all my own, with additional information spliced in by Peter Hands. I have tried to point out anything unusual in view but I make no claim to be an authority on the period or the areas. Memory being what it is, if you disagree with my identification, you are probably right. Many aspects of the railway scene have changed since these pictures were taken, so if I have not commented on something which was once commonplace but now rare because it has gone, then please forgive me. I hope you will enjoy reading through this album. Peter Hay - July 1989.

If you feel that you have suitable material of BR steam locomotives between 1948-1968 and wish to contribute them towards future albums please contact — Peter Hands, 190 Yoxall Road, Shirley, Solihull, West Midlands B90 3RN.

CONTENTS

1)   SR H2 Class 4-4-2 No 32425 *Trevose Head.*
(Peter Hay)

2)   SR I3 Class 4-4-2T No 32091 works plate.
(Peter Hay)

3)   GWR *Castle* Class 4-6-0 No 4088 *Dartmouth Castle.* (G.W. Sharpe)

4)   GWR *Star* Class 4-6-0 No 4035 *Queen Charlotte.* (Peter Hay)

5) Generations of cross-channel passengers have leaned out of carriage windows, wondering about the delay whilst their train stood in the reversing sidings at Folkestone Junction station, and this was often what they saw. SR R1 Class 0-6-0T No 31047 (74C Dover) was for years one of the incline pilots, though by May 1957 it was nearing the end of its life, being withdrawn from 70A Nine Elms in March 1960. (Peter Hay)

6)   Dumpton Park station, between Broadstairs and Ramsgate, was built by the SR in 1926, when railways at Ramsgate were rationalised. SR *Schools* Class 4-4-0 No 30908 *Westminster,* from 73A Stewarts Lane, heads the 4.15 pm Ramsgate to Victoria on 3rd September 1958, past weed-strewn surplus land never needed for a second island platform. The third rail is already in position. (Peter Hay)

7)   Hordes of enthusiasts disgorge at Margate from the coaches of an S.L.S. special on 19th May 1957. Such was the professional skill of the driver, Sam Gingell, that SR D1 Class 4-4-0 No 31545 (73A Stewarts Lane) has stopped exactly by the water crane, despite the fact that at Westgate, a mere 1½ miles away, it had been travelling at over 60 mph. An exciting start to the rail-tour. (Peter Hay)

8) In 1952 many Kent Coast expresses were worked by the then new SR *Battle of Britain* Class 4-6-2's shedded at 74B Ramsgate. Photographed on shed in April 1952 are SR C Class 0-6-0 No 31004, behind which is an unrebuilt *B of B* version No 34076 41 *Squadron*. Alongside 31004 is the distinctive tender of another *Battle of Britain* Class member. Ramsgate bade farewell to its allocation of Pacifics in June 1959. (Peter Hay)

9) Somebody on the shed staff at Ramsgate cared enough for the local carriage pilot, SR H Class 0-4-4T No 31521, to polish its splasher beading and works-plate. The unlettered tank side and SR numerals indicate a date of around 1950 for this picture. The pre-war Maunsell Restaurant Car next to the locomotive has the S prefix to its number. No 31521 survived in service until May 1962 being withdrawn from 75F Tunbridge Wells. (Peter Hay)

10) On 23rd May 1959 the Railway Enthusiasts Club ran a railtour of East Kent, seen here standing at Minster. The contents of the van are unknown but the immaculately turned out SR O1 Class 0-6-0 No 31258 was one of the last survivors of the once numerous class, then shedded at 74C Dover for working over the former East Kent Light Railway. No 31258 demised in February 1961. (Peter Hay)

11) BRITISH RAILWAYS on the tender of SR C Class 0-6-0 No 31298 indicates that this picture was taken after nationalisation, a fact confirmed by the presence of a wooden bodied former private owner's coal wagon behind the tender. On the right is an ex. LSWR coach, numbered DS 1595, part of the breakdown train then based at 74B. No 31298 ended its days based at 73C Hither Green. (Peter Hay)

12) This train leaving Ramsgate on 7th September 1958 is not empty stock but the 12.40 pm local working to Dover which will reverse at Minster. A less than clean SR *King Arthur* Class 4-6-0 No 30768 *Sir Balin* (73A Stewarts Lane), working tender-first, provided the motive power, hauling some of the narrow, slab-sided SR stock which was built for the Hastings line in 1933. (Peter Hay)

13) Having arrived at Minster with the 12.40 pm Ramsgate to Dover, *Sir Balin,* with safety valves roaring, has run round its train and waits for the starting signal to be cleared so that it can resume its journey. No 30768 was withdrawn from 71A Eastleigh in October 1961 and cut up shortly afterwards. (Peter Hay)

14)   In April 1952 the weather in Kent was still cold enough for the guard to keep his stove alight in the second vehicle of this van train at Ramsgate. SR D1 Class 4-4-0 No 31505, from 73A Stewarts Lane, couldn't provide steam heating because of the goods van next to the tender. No 31505 was transferred away from Kent, to 70A Nine Elms in June 1959, where it eked out an existence until condemned in September 1961. (Peter Hay)

15)   A local train from Dover approaches Minster, in Thanet, on 7th September 1958. The engine is LMS-type Class 4 2-6-4T No 42092, seen in filthy external condition. No 42092 was one of a number of the class constructed at Brighton Works and originally allocated to the Southern Region. It was drafted to the London Midland Region in December 1959. (Peter Hay)

16)   Two ladies and a porter await the arrival of BR Class 4 2-6-4T No 80011 (75F Tunbridge Wells) as it glides into Walmer, between Deal and Dover on 6th September 1958. The roofboards on the two leading coaches of this train show that they are the Dover and Ramsgate portion of the 7.35 am from Birkenhead, a train that contrived to serve almost every holiday resort in south Sussex and Kent. (Peter Hay)

17)   As LMS-type Class 4 2-6-4T No 42075, a Dover locomotive, stops at Martin Mill (for St. Margarets Bay) the fireman has put the injector on to prevent his engine blowing off. The carriages are Southern Railway but on the left there is something older: Ex. SECR bogies, in use as Camping coaches on 7th September 1958. No 42075 left the Southern for pastures new in December 1959, being drafted to 1A Willesden. (Peter Hay)

18)   BR Mk 1 carriages precede a Maunsell SR Buffet Car in the train behind a smartly turned out SR Rebuilt *West Country* Class
      4-6-2 No 34005 *Barnstaple,* allocated to 73B Bricklayers Arms, as it stops at Martin Mill on 6th September 1958, on the former
      Dover & Deal Joint line. Duty No 467 was a Margate to London service. Ousted from Kent Coast duties in January 1961,
      Barnstaple moved on to 72B Salisbury. (Peter Hay)

19)   SR *King Arthur* Class 4-6-0 No 30797 *Sir Blamor de Ganis* (74C Dover) passes a down train as it calls to collect passengers
      from Sandling station, whilst working a Ramsgate to Charing Cross service on 20th July 1957. With the closure of the Hythe
      branch in 1951, Sandling was no longer a junction and was somewhat reduced in importance. *Sir Blamor de Ganis* was reduced
      to scrap at Eastleigh Works in June 1959. (A.E. Bennett)

20)   After the high speed dash from London, a railtour over the former East Kent Light Railway to Eythorne, was taken at a very sedate pace with SR O1 Class 0-6-0's at each end of the train. 74C Dover based No 31434, specially turned out for the occasion, stands alongside the timber faced platform at Eythorne on 19th May 1957. No 31434 was condemned in August 1959 from Dover shed, being cut up the same month. (A.E. Bennett)

21)   One of the rare SR E2 Class 0-6-0 Tanks, No 32109 was shedded at Dover for many years. Attention was being paid to the locomotive as it stood in the depot yard in 1952. The design was virtually in the 'as built' condition, apart from the addition of vacuum brake equipment. Only the front numberplate tells of BR ownership. No 32109 moved to 71I Southampton Docks in January 1957 being withdrawn from there in April 1963. (Peter Hay)

22) The empty stock for this boat train to Victoria has been brought into the Marine station at Dover on 19th May 1957, by H Class 0-4-4T No 31542, a local engine. It had been freshly repainted but because of the shortage of cleaners during the peak summer traffic, it had already become grubby, with the SECR works-plate on the splasher unpolished. Surplus to requirements at Dover, No 31542 moved to 70A Nine Elms in July 1960. (Peter Hay)

23) Dover shed, 74C, built on reclaimed land in 1928, is home in April 1952 to SR L Class 4-4-0 No 31780. The engine had been painted in malachite green, with BRITISH RAILWAYS and its number in gold blocked letters. The penultimate member of the class, No 31780 was reallocated to 70A Nine Elms from 73G Ramsgate in June 1959 and withdrawn from the former shed in July 1961, being scrapped at Ashford Works. (Peter Hay)

24) An extremely smart SR C Class 0-6-0 No 31113 has steam to spare at Dover in April 1952 at the head of an oil tanker train. In the background is sister engine No 31150, both being allocated to the local shed. Behind No 31150, French vans are being shunted onto the Dunkirk train ferry, which is hidden by the signal gantry spanning these busy tracks. (Peter Hay)

25) The platform and building behind SR D1 Class 4-4-0 No 31487, were once the South Eastern Railway station of Dover Town, closed in 1914. In the foreground are the railings round the 65 foot turntable of 74C Dover shed, with the Victorian fortifications of the Western Heights in the distance. No 31487 ended its days at 73B Bricklayers Arms in February 1961 and was put to the torch at Ashford Works. (Peter Hay)

26) A highly polished SR R1 Class 0-6-0T No 31107 (74C Dover) has brought this train down to the Harbour station at Folkestone on 19th May 1957. Judging by the number of people on the tracks, the boarded-over rails seem to be an invitation to jump down from the platform rather than use the footbridge. No 31107 was yet another Kentish locomotive which was drafted to 70A Nine Elms in 1959. (Peter Hay)

27) The plume from the safety valves shows that SR C Class 0-6-0 No 31720 (73H Dover) is in fact steaming *off* the South Coast, for the engine is afloat. On 21st February 1960 it was on board the train ferry *SS Shepperton Ferry* at Dover, about to draw some continental ferry vans onto English rails. Transferred to 73F Ashford in May 1961, No 31720 was condemned five months later. (Peter Hay)

28) During 1957 the *Golden Arrow* ran from Victoria to Folkestone and then the Pullmans were worked empty to Dover for the return trip in the afternoon. Such a heavy train required no less than four of the SR R1 Class 0-6-0 Tanks, in tandem at either end, to climb the 1 in 30 to the Junction station, as this and the next picture show on 19th July 1957. The second engine can be identified as No 31340 (74C). (A.E. Bennett)

29) This is the rear of the empty *Golden Arrow* train leaving Folkestone Harbour. The apparent gap between the last Pullman and the van in front of the bankers, Nos 31047 and 31107, is occupied by a flat truck which had carried the Registered Luggage containers, now on board ship, down from London. Like No 31340, both of the bankers were also based at 74C Dover, but were sub-shedded at Folkestone. (A.E. Bennett)

30) GWR 5700 Class 0-6-0 Pannier Tanks took over the battle with the 1 in 30 incline up from Folkestone Harbour during 1959. No 4631 is almost at the summit with an eleven coach train, including two Pullman cars on 3rd May 1959. No 4631 had been transferred to 73H Dover in January 1959 from 88E Abercynon and it remained there until September 1961 from where it went to 73A Stewarts Lane. (A.E. Bennett)

31) Quite what SR *King Arthur* Class 4-6-0 No 30796 *Sir Dodinas le Savage,* from 73C Hither Green was doing on the 5.20 pm Ramsgate to Victoria service on 1st September 1958, only the shed foreman could explain. However it seemed to be making good progress with the train, photographed near Walmer. When the electrics began using these tracks, the engine was transferred to 72B Salisbury for the remainder of its working life. (Peter Hay)

32) A regular weekday job for a 'Brighton Atlantic' was the run to Bournemouth (West) and back, arriving home in time for tea. On a bright winter's morning, in December 1957, SR H2 Class 4-4-2 No 32424 *Beachy Head* envelopes Hove station with smoke and steam as it hustles through with its lightweight load. However, the writing was on the wall for these famous locomotives, with extinction on the immediate horizon. (Peter Hay)

33) In this busy scene at Hastings on 14th August 1955, admiring crowds on the platform turn their backs on SR L Class 4-4-0 No 31764 as SR E1 Class 4-4-0 No 31019 (73A Stewarts Lane) and SR D Class 4-4-0 No 31737 (now preserved) make their way to St. Leonards shed after working a railtour from Tonbridge. No 31764 was withdrawn in February 1961 with No 31019 faring little better, following on two months later. (Peter Hay)

34) This gathering in the shed yard at 74E St. Leonards, on 26th August 1956, is representative of engine types long associated with the place and the lines it served. On the left is SR *Schools* Class 4-4-0 No 30924 *Haileybury,* whilst the other tender engine is SR L Class 4-4-0 No 31765. The other two engines are SR H Class 0-4-4 Tanks, No 31307 in the centre, both of which worked local services. (A.E. Bennett)

35) The Tonbridge - Hastings route has seen not one but two changes of traction since this view of Bopeep Junction at St. Leonards was taken on 24th April 1957. SR L1 Class 4-4-0 No 31786 has just restarted from West St. Leonards with a Saturday 'stopper' from Sevenoaks. Bopeep Junction is where the line from Charing Cross via Tonbridge (left) joins the East Coastway from Brighton before entering Hastings. (Peter Hay)

36) Lewes is in the distance and the electric rails have been left behind as the fireman on SR D1 Class 4-4-0 No 31492, a 74D Tonbridge locomotive, makes up his fire before the next stop at Barcombe Mills. The train is the 4.36 pm from Brighton to Tonbridge. No 31492 was destined to remain on the books at Tonbridge shed until condemned in January 1960. Cutting up occurred at Ashford Works a month later. (Peter Hay)

37) A 'Vulcan' or SR C2X Class 0-6-0 No 32438 demonstrating the ups and downs of branch line service between Barcombe and Culver Junction, on the Lewes to East Grinstead line, in August 1956. The two coach LBSCR 'motor' set was the accomodation at first provided when the service over this line was compulsorily reinstated in accordance with the original Act. Note the double dome boiler as applied to No 32438. (Peter Hay)

38) Coal trains are not common in Sussex but this one approaching Pevensey is a regular working. Supplies for Galley Hill gasworks at Bexhill were imported through Newhaven and on this occasion makes the last stage of the journey, in June 1959, behind SR K Class 2-6-0 No 32343, based at 75A Brighton. Withdrawn from Brighton in December 1962, No 32343 was not cut up until late in 1964 at King's, Norwich. (Peter Hay)

39)   A local service operated for many years between Eastbourne and Hailsham, perhaps a relic of the time when both stations were at the end of branches and the same branch train served both. In June 1959 a well groomed SR K Class 2-6-0 No 32348, from 75E Three Bridges, is in charge approaching Hampden Park. Condemned in November 1962, No 32348 was scrapped at Eastleigh Works a month later. (Peter Hay)

40)   The SR C2X Class 0-6-0's were a twentieth century rebuild of a Victorian design, which produced a useful increase in power. No 32540, from 75A Brighton, is seen from an unusual angle at Newhaven shed in May 1953. Behind No 32540 stands the real answer to the LBSCR heavy goods problem, the K Class 2-6-0, represented by No 32350 built in 1920, which had a life span of some forty-two years. (Peter Hay)

41) Photographs can sometimes remind us of a distinctive sound and anyone who has heard a Bulleid Pacific in original condition pulling away after a stop will know exactly what this scene sounded like and recognise the unique exhaust pattern: dollops of steam rolling out, rather than a sharp beat. SR *Battle of Britain* Class 4-6-2 No 34088 *213 Squadron* leaves Patcham Tunnel on the main line from Brighton in February 1952. (Peter Hay)

42) Brighton to Tunbridge Wells trains did not stop at Falmer, between Brighton and Lewes, in steam days, so SR E4 Class 0-6-2T No 32581 (75F Tunbridge Wells), its appearance highlighted by bright sunshine, was keeping on the move as it neared the station and the top of the three mile climb from Brighton. On 16th October 1958, a pre-war SR corridor set was the load. (Peter Hay)

43)   This is a locospotter's view of 75A Brighton shed on 17th October 1955 where all the engines on view were of Southern origin. Right to left are: T9 Class 4-4-0 No 30310, P Class 0-6-0T No 31556, E2 Class 0-6-0T No 32105 and an unidentified *King Arthur* Class 4-6-0. On the wheel drop sidings to the left are M7 Class 0-4-4T No 30129 and K Class 2-6-0 No 32345. At the time pre-Grouping classes like this were quite common. (Peter Hay)

44)   At first glance it looks as if there is something amiss with this photograph. This picture shows the first appearance of the ill-fated 'Leader' Class 0-6-6-0T outside Brighton Works on 21st June 1949. It was as yet un-numbered and in grey works paint. Coal in the bunker can just be seen at the left hand end. (H.M. Madgwick)

45)   One must forgive the poor quality of this particular picture as photographs of 'Leader' locomotives on the move are few. A by now begrimed example of the 0-6-6-0 Tanks No 36001 arrives at Brighton in the summer of 1949 after a trial trip on the Lewes line, with a scratch collection of old carriages and vans. (H.M. Madgwick)

46)   The uncompleted third member of the 'Leader' Class never carried its number of 36003. This is the smokebox end, the white 'wall' further from the camera being beside the bunker. Alongside No 36003, outside Brighton Works on 20th May 1951 is a brand new LMS-type Class 4 2-6-4T No 42094, which was destined to remain in service for just over eleven years being surplus to requirements in October 1962. (H.M. Madgwick)

47) Escaping steam outlines the shapely and unusual chimney as fitted to SR E5 Class 0-6-2T No 32406, in excellent external condition. Apart from livery changes and pop valves the engine is virtually as it was built in 1904. In April 1951 it is seen departing in a flurry of steam from Brighton with a Tunbridge Wells train. Just four months away from withdrawal, 32406 never carried the BR emblem. (Peter Hay)

48) An interloper on the Southern. LMS Stanier Class 5 4-6-0 No 45097 from 1A Willesden, nearing the end of its journey from Watford with a Sunday excursion to Brighton in August 1962, passing Preston Park, the last station before Brighton. Strangely the first three coaches are of GWR, LMS and LNER designs. Note also the smartly maintained platforms at Preston Park. (Peter Hay)

49) During 1951 Brighton Works built LMR-type Class 4 2-6-4 Tanks, many of which, including No 42093 seen here, were allocated to local sheds to replace old engines which were being scrapped. In May 1952, 42093 works a Saturday through train to the Western Region, giving Preston Park and district the benefit of a smoke-screen. No 42093 later found its way onto the North Eastern Region being condemned in October 1967. (Peter Hay)

50) The similarity between Maunsell's rebuild of the former SECR D and E Class 4-4-0's into D1 and E1 and his first 4-4-0 design for the SR, Class L1, will be obvious if this picture is compared with photograph number 36. L1 Class No 31785, from 73D Gillingham is passing the site of the first Falmer station at the top of the 1 in 88 climb from Lewes, with 11.08 am Redhill to Brighton in May 1957. (Peter Hay)

51) This excursion returning to the LMR Western Division, the old LNWR section, seemed to be following the hard pounding, fire throwing tradition of that Company as it climbed through the South Downs north of Patcham Tunnel, on the exit from Brighton, in May 1952. The engine is LMS Class 5 4-6-0 No 45071 and so is all of the stock except the first coach, which is an LNWR composite with a luggage van at each end. (Peter Hay)

52) Traffic on the Horsham - Brighton line grew to such an extent in the 1950's, that three coach push and pull trains were necessary. On 28th May 1956, SR M7 Class 0-4-4T No 30051 is running alongside the river Adur at Shoreham, just before joining the West Coastway line. The three coaches consist of two LBSCR carriages and one Southern Railway. No 30051 was to survive in service a further six years or so. (Peter Hay)

53) The 11.33 am Lancing empty stock train consisted of a piebald collection of vans and coaches newly painted at Lancing Works on 30th July 1954. It formed a heavy load for SR L Class 4-4-0 No 31765 as it headed for East Croydon through Hove. Hove station is in the distance and the engine faced a short but heavily curved climb at 1 in 90, up to Preston Park. (Peter Hay)

54) In direct contrast to the previous picture, SR U1 Class 2-6-0 No 31906 based at 73A Stewarts Lane has steam to spare as it coasts down the Cliftonville Spur from Preston Park to Hove on 28th July 1954. The train is a Sunday excursion from the Western Region, bound for Worthing and Littlehampton. No 31906 was withdrawn from active service from 75C Norwood Junction in December 1962. (Peter Hay)

55) The SR D3 Class 0-4-4 Tanks were for many years the mainstay of the Brighton to Horsham services, after the scrapping of the Stroudley D1 Class 0-4-2 Tanks. No 32390 was for some time the last D3 and is seen here departing from Portslade with the 2.25 pm Brighton to Horsham train on 25th April 1953. The carriages are vintage ex. London and South Western Railway. (Peter Hay)

56) This veteran assemblage approaching Shoreham is the daily special for employees, between Brighton and Lancing Carriage Works. Various rakes of old carriages were employed down the years; in the 1950's the train was composed of 1890's LSWR stock. On 10th May 1956, the engine being used is SR E4 Class 0-6-2T No 32485 from Brighton, which was condemned a few months after this picture was taken. (Peter Hay)

57) SR D Class 4-4-0 No 31737 was selected for preservation when it was withdrawn from service in 1956. Two years earlier it was still out and about on the occasional main line duty, as this photograph taken in August 1954 bears witness to. No 31737 is hauling the Hastings - Birkenhead through train, just to the north of Brighton, near Preston Park. (Peter Hay)

58) Students of locomotive detail will find much to note in the appearance of SR A1X Class 0-6-0T No DS 680, one of the Lancing Carriage Works pilots in November 1955. For a start, although an A1X, it retained its smokebox wingplates. Its non-standard looks, unusual even for this much altered class, were relics of four different owners since 1876. In company with DS 680 is SR E4 Class 0-6-2T No 32577. (Peter Hay)

59)   By 1955 the wharf at Littlehampton could only stand the weight of the SR A1X Class 0-6-0 Tanks, here represented by No 32661. Coupled to it is a brake van reserved for local traffic between Chichester, Arundel and Littlehampton in December 1955. Condemned from 71A Eastleigh in April 1963, No 32661 languished in store there until the call of the cutter's torch came in August of the same year. (Peter Hay)

60)   A lighted headlamp rather than a white disc on the front of SR Q Class 0-6-0 No 30544 shows that the daylight will be gone before this up van train reached its destination. It is hurrying along the West Coastway line near Ford in May 1956, when antiques like the leading vehicle, an elderly 6-wheeled full brake, were still thought fit to run. No 30544 itself continued to run until January 1964. (Peter Hay)

61)   SR K Class 2-6-0 No 32353 has just crossed the bridge over the river Arun at Ford with a goods working from Horsham and the Mid-Sussex line to Chichester in May 1956. The bridge lost its ability to open for river traffic as far back as 1938, whilst the sidings which once served rail/river transhipment (in the foreground) had disappeared many years before that. (Peter Hay)

62)   We leave Sussex with a photograph of the 1.50 pm Bournemouth (West) to Brighton service which has just come over the hump in the track at Ford caused by the bridge over the river Arun. SR H2 Class 4-4-2 No 32425 *Trevose Head* has the usual weekday formation of a Maunsell 3-set and a Bulleid 'swinger' on 16th May 1956, an easy day's work for a Brighton 'Atlantic'. (Peter Hay)

63) No 30300, a 71A Eastleigh locomotive, was one of the last batch of SR T9 Class 4-4-0's, with full-width splashers. On 9th July 1957 it was heading home to Eastleigh, through Porchester, with the 4.03 pm passenger from Portsmouth. Withdrawn from Eastleigh in March 1961 it was reduced to scrap at the nearby works the following month. (Peter Hay)

64) A photographer standing on the track would normally get a picture which showed most engines towering over him but the SR A1X Class 0-6-0 Tanks were so small that the low viewpoint is not obtrusive. Here is No 32650, now preserved on the Kent & East Sussex Railway, in between trips to Hayling Island, standing in the bay platform at Havant in August 1954. No 32650 was withdrawn in November 1963. (Peter Hay)

65) The 31st August 1954 had been a fine sunny day for holidaymakers and photographers alike and as the evening shadows lengthened, a faithful but unidentified SR A1X Class 0-6-0T sets off, bunker-first, with four packed LSWR bogies from Hayling Island to Havant. (Peter Hay)

66)   The pre-war Maunsell brake third towered over SR A1X Class 0-6-0T No 32677, allocated to 71D Fratton, as it left North Hayling in April 1953. This locomotive was reputed to be the very last to carry a genuine Stroudley chimney with a copper cap. No 32677 was condemned from Fratton in September 1959 and destroyed at Eastleigh Works in May 1960. (Peter Hay)

67)   There actually is an engine at the head of this train approaching Langston Bridge on the Hayling Island branch. As normal it is a SR A1X Class 0-6-0T, so small as to be invisible in front of the LSWR carriage from which the picture was taken, in August 1954. The 'both ways' signal is a home signal for the swing bridge and Langston Crossing's up distant. On the right is the former train ferry berth to Brading. (Peter Hay)

68)   SR T9 Class 4-4-0's like No 30285 always looked well from a low viewpoint. This rail level picture shows an evening train
        from Eastleigh to Portsmouth approaching Cosham on 8th April 1955. The writing was on the wall for No 30285 with withdrawal
        looming in June 1958. In common with many other members of the class it was dismantled at Eastleigh Works, in this case
        during the same month as withdrawal. (Peter Hay)

69)   A parting look at the Hayling Island branch. In contrast to the half hourly service, four coach trains and non-stop runs on
        summer Saturdays, in the winter things were pretty quiet. At Hayling Island, on 3rd April 1953, SR A1X Class 0-6-0T No
        32677 has only one coach and not many customers. (Peter Hay)

70) One of the much admired and spruced up Brighton 'Atlantics', SR H2 Class 4-4-2 No 32425 *Trevose Head,* restarts from Fratton with a railtour on 3rd May 1953. The leading coach is second class, from a boat train, at a time when there was still third class accomodation. (Peter Hay)

71) The meagre service of passenger trains on the Fawley branch came to an end on 14th February 1966. Hythe was the only branch station with a water tank, though by 11th June 1957 there was no sign of the water column which once stood at the side of the line. SR M7 Class 0-4-4T No 30032, from 71A Eastleigh, is working the afternoon train from Southampton. (A.E. Bennett)

72) Hardly the correct express passenger power for the Portsmouth portion of the Cardiff through train in July 1955. SR C2X Class 0-6-0 No 32548 bustles along with four bogies near Fareham. The main portion of the train had gone on ahead to Brighton behind a *West Country* Pacific. Notice the two domes: the front one was a shell, remaining after an early top feed experiment. (Peter Hay)

73) This 1951 picture at 71D Fratton shows one of the SR H15 Class 4-6-0's, No 30334, almost at the end of its days. No 30334 had started its life as one of the unsuccessful Drummond 4-6-0's, being rebuilt to something more useful by his successor. Its career finished in June 1958 when it was taken out of service from 72B Salisbury, being cut up at Eastleigh the following month. (G.W. Sharpe)

74) Well cleaned in the lined black British Railways livery with the first BR emblem on the eight-wheeled 'water-cart' tender, SR T9 Class 'Greyhound' 4-4-0 No 30730 has a clear road ahead as it pulls out of the low level platforms at Portsmouth & Southsea, with a train for Southampton via Netley on the afternoon of 20th May 1955. No 30730, a 70F Fratton engine, was withdrawn from there in August 1957. (Peter Hay)

75) We now switch our attentions to the Isle of Wight where we find SR 02 Class 0-4-4T No 27 *Merstone* on the summer only double track between Ryde and Smallbrook Junction. In September 1952 it is working a four coach train for Newport and Cowes, with ex. SECR mainland stock. In BR days engines on the island still had painted bufferbeam numbers, here in SR style. (Peter Hay)

76)   Few stations were closer to the South Coast than Ventnor West, which closed in 1952. In 1949 it was still served by trains from Merstone Junction on the Newport to Sandown line. Behind the LBSCR brake composite, one of the trusty Isle of Wight SR O2 Class 0-4-4 Tanks waits for its next scheduled departure. (N.W. Sprinks)

77)   SR O2 Class 0-4-4T No 14 *Fishbourne* was the last regular engine working the Bembridge branch and here on 18th May 1952 it sweeps round to the junction at Brading with a packed railtour. The LBSCR 'motor' set was the normal stock on the branch but the unhappy lining of *Fishbourne's* bunker was confined to this engine alone. *Fishbourne* survived in service until December 1966. (Peter Hay)

78)   After the closure of the branches to Ventnor West and Bembridge in 1952 and 1953, there was a surplus of engines on the Isle of Wight. SR 02 Class 0-4-4 Tanks Nos 23 *Totland* and 19 *Osborne* were stored, never to work again, late in 1955 at 71F Ryde. Despite the fact that they were protected with properly secured chimney caps and wooden shutters to keep the winter rain out of the cabs they were soon cut up. (Peter Hay)

79)   With the gleaming red ex. LBSCR saloon next to the engine, SR E1 Class 0-6-0T No 3 *Ryde,* prepares to depart from Cowes with an early railtour of the island lines on 18th May 1952. Today there is no trace of this once busy station which closed in December 1966. The locomotive *Ryde* was withdrawn from 70H Ryde shed in July 1959. (Peter Hay)

80) As soon as it became available again after the Second World War, malachite green paint was applied to engines on the Isle of Wight. This picture of SR 02 Class 0-4-4T No 32 *Bonchurch* standing at Freshwater in May 1952, shows how well it wore. BRITISH RAILWAYS is in a style unique to the Isle of Wight but the engine's number is pure Southern Railway. (Peter Hay)

81) This grass-grown location was once occupied by Paulsgrove Halt, between Cosham and Porchester. It served Portsmouth Racecourse, and this picture of an evening train to Eastleigh, headed by SR T9 Class 4-4-0 No 30724, is taken from the site of the grandstand in July 1955. No 30724 was taken out of service from 70C Guildford in May 1959 and broken up at Eastleigh a month later. (Peter Hay)

82)   Another 'Greyhound' on active service. The 4.08 pm Brockenhurst to Portsmouth has just climbed the 1 in 81 from Bursledon to Swanwick with a 5 car set of Bulleid-type coaches as the load for SR T9 Class 4-4-0 No 30283 (71A Eastleigh). No doubt the fireman of No 30283 had put down his shovel now that the mountaineering was over, much of his day's work done on 9th July 1957. (Peter Hay)

83)   The down *Bournemouth Belle* on 18th June 1955 was composed of 11 Pullman cars weighing nearly 500 tons. Here it is coasting through St. Denys with steam shut off, two miles from its first stop at Southampton (Central) with SR Unrebuilt *Merchant Navy* Class 4-6-2 No 35017 *Belgian Marine* in charge. Constructed in April 1945, No 35017 was rebuilt at Eastleigh in March 1957, ten years before withdrawal. (Peter Hay)

84) This fine former London & South Western Railway ensemble at Southampton Terminus station (closed in 1966),is composed of SR M7 Class 0-4-4T No 30040, built in 1898, with some contemporary carriages. In June 1955 it was working the twice daily train to Fawley on the far side of Southampton Water. For the latter years of its working life it was based at 71B Bournemouth until withdrawn in June 1961. (Peter Hay)

85) Although many regretted the passing from the Southampton Docks scene of the older four wheeled engines, their successors continued the tradition of 'something different' in the docks. Purchased virtually unused and a bargain at £2,500 each, some of the USA Class 0-6-0 Tanks saw out the end of steam on the Southern. No 30072 pauses in its shunting duties beside the Channel Islands passenger terminal on 18th June 1955. (Peter Hay)

86)   Although built for and best known on the London - Hastings services, both before and after World War II, the SR *Schools* Class 4-4-0's also worked on the Bournemouth line. With condemnation four short months away No 30937 *Epsom* is photographed leaving Southampton (Central) with a heavy train bound for Portsmouth. Bulleid set No 814 built at Eastleigh in 1948 leads BR Mk I stock on 4th August 1962. (J.H.W. Kent)

87)   Such is the shine on SR U Class 2-6-0 No 31809 from 71A Eastleigh, that it surely must have been repainted shortly before being captured on camera on 4th August 1962. No 31809 is departing from Southampton (Central) with a Bournemouth line train consisting of Western Region stock. Re-allocated to 70C Guildford in June 1964, No 31809 was to soldier on there until the end came in January 1966. (A.E. Bennett)

88)   As older engines were scrapped, BR Class 4 2-6-0's like No 76019 allocated to 71A Eastleigh, took over local workings in East Hampshire. This is a Portsmouth to Salisbury train calling at Netley, between Fareham and Southampton, on 7th July 1957. Before withdrawal in February 1966, No 76019 was to serve at Salisbury and Bournemouth sheds before returning for a final fling at Eastleigh. (Peter Hay)

89)   Photographed from a low viewpoint SR Rebuilt *Merchant Navy* Class 4-6-2 No 35020 *Bibby Line,* based at 70A Nine Elms, heads a down Waterloo to Bournemouth express away from Brockenhurst in the New Forest and up the sharp rise after Lymington Junction on a misty 10th June 1963. A road bridge on the branch to Lymington can be seen on the extreme right. *Bibby Line* was rebuilt in May 1959. (Peter Hay)

90) The train passing Lymington Junction is the 5.34 pm Eastleigh to Bournemouth (West) service, running via the now closed line through Ringwood. Brockenhurst station is round the corner to the left, the Lymington branch goes off to the right in front of the signalbox — note the tablet-catcher. On 10th June 1963 the motive power was BR Class 4 2-6-0 No 76016, from 71A Eastleigh. (Peter Hay)

91) It would be difficult (but not impossible — see picture No 27) to get closer to the South Coast than at Lymington Pier. Late on a June evening in 1963, SR M7 Class 0-4-4T No 30057 waits to work the last train of the day to Brockenhurst on the main line. Because of restricted clearance with the siding on the right, the signal arms were unusually short. No 30057 was withdrawn during this same month. (Peter Hay)

92) A tail lamp on the bufferbeam shows that SR M7 Class 0-4-4T No 30052 (71B Bournemouth) is pushing its train as it braked to a halt at Lymington Town on 10th June 1963. Happily, this branch in Hampshire still has trains, though the all-over roof of the station has since been removed. No 30052 had been transferred to Bournemouth shed from 72C Yeovil in April 1963. (Peter Hay)

93) New Milton had a typical LSWR 'glasshouse' signalbox of the 1880's, dating in fact from 1888 and in 1965 the occupant has a close-up view of SR Rebuilt *Merchant Navy* Class 4-6-2 No 35013 *Blue Funnel,* from 70F Bournemouth, as it arrives with a Bournemouth to Waterloo service. The train watchers would have had plenty to look at as we can just make out the tail of a down train in the distance. (J.H.W. Kent)

94)   Moving away from Hampshire and on into Dorset, the chapter commences with a fine overhead view of the yard at 71G Weymouth in June 1961, where former GWR and SR locomotives were once a common sight. SR Unrebuilt *West Country* Class 4-6-2 No 34043 *Coombe Martin* (71B Bournemouth) is in company with GWR *Grange* Class 4-6-0 No 6841 *Marlas Grange* (82B St. Philip's Marsh). Note that the three original safety valves on No 34043 had been reduced to two and moved nearer to the cab. (C.H. Attwell)

95)   An up express from Weymouth passes Christchurch, with a Gresley LNER brake leading the train in August 1965. SR Rebuilt *West Country* Class 4-6-2 No 34034 *Honiton* has lost its name and numberplates, though a home-made replacement for the latter has been fitted to the smokebox. Built in July 1946, *Honiton* was rebuilt in August 1960 and condemned from 70A Nine Elms in July 1967. (J.H.W. Kent)

96)   BR Class 5 4-6-0 No 73169, a 70D Eastleigh locomotive, approaches Boscombe with a gleaming train of Bulleid's distinctive carriages in 1965. Signalling is all semaphore and there is no sign of the electrification that would sweep away steam traction within two years. No 73169 started its life in April 1957 at 50A York and ended it at Eastleigh in October 1966 — what a waste!!! (J.H.W. Kent)

97) The down platform at Bournemouth (Central) extended past the locomotive depot giving the enthusiast many 'bonus' photographs right up until the end of steam at the shed. SR Rebuilt *Battle of Britain* Class 4-6-2 No 34082 *615 Squadron,* a visitor from 70A Nine Elms, had just left the shed on 9th July 1964, in readiness to take over a down working. Note the impressive signal gantry. (Alan Jones)

98) A begrimed BR Class 4 4-6-0 No 75073, based at 83G Templecombe and equipped with a double chimney, stands in bright sunshine on station pilot duty at Bournemouth (Central) in October 1963. It is said that the top glass from the all-over roof was removed because Bulleid Pacifics blowing off steam at 280 lbs. per square inch were showering passengers with glass. (J.H.W. Kent)

99) An impressive photograph taken from the fifth coach of an up train as it squealed over the heavily check-railed curves preceding Gas Works Junction at Bournemouth. This service started at Bournemouth (West) and is heading for Waterloo via the Central station behind an unidentified SR Unrebuilt *West Country* Class 4-6-2 in the summer of 1965. This curve and the West station closed that autumn. (J.H.W. Kent)

100) Engines off Somerset & Dorset workings were serviced at Branksome, a sub-shed of 71B Bournemouth which hosted, in the main, locomotives based at Bath Green Park and Templecombe. LMS Class 2P 4-4-0 No 40601 from the former shed is being serviced at Branksome on an unknown day in 1958 and no doubt it needed a refilled tender after crossing the Mendips. This engine was withdrawn in December 1959. (A.C. Ingram)

101) The lamp headcode (instead of discs) indicates that BR Class 4 4-6-0 No 75008, from 83G Templecombe, but bereft of shedplate, is working an S & D service through Parkstone on 29th August 1964. Signs of the times includes electrification 'flashes' on the engine and the coloured strip over the 'first class' section of the third vehicle. No 75008 had acquired its double chimney in September 1962. (J.H.W. Kent)

102) SR *King Arthur* Class 4-6-0 No 30763 *Sir Bors de Ganis* nearing the end of its career whilst working Nine Elms duty No 42, a down Weymouth express, pulls out of Poole station in the summer of 1959. This station was virtually a compulsory stop for all passenger trains. Despite sporting a 71A Eastleigh shedplate, records show that No 30763 was based at 70A Nine Elms from August 1957 to September 1960. (J.H.W. Kent)

103)   After the diesel takeover of the Hastings line, some SR *Schools* 4-4-0's enjoyed a 'swan-song' on the Bournemouth and Weymouth services. No 30909 *St. Paul's* was on loan from 73A Stewarts Lane when it appeared at Poole in July 1958. Equipped with a multiple jet blastpipe and large diameter chimney, *St. Paul's* was drafted from Stewarts Lane to pastures new at 70A Nine Elms, in June 1959. (J.H.W. Kent)

104)   LMS Class 4F 0-6-0 No 44559 was constructed as Somerset & Dorset Joint Railway No 59 in 1922 and on 18th July 1957 it was still working on the S & D section, based at 82F Bath Green Park. As it leaves Poole there are two peculiarities to note: the tablet exchanger sticking out of the tender front and the special lamp headcode used by all trains on the S & D. No 44559 demised from Green Park in November 1962. (J.H.W. Kent)

105) Looking east towards Holes Bay Junction we see the somewhat unlikely sight of SR Q1 Class 0-6-0 No 33007, from 70B Feltham, hauling a train of LNER Gresley stock on 18th July 1959. Neither the headcode (incorrect) nor the allocation of the engine to Feltham, (shedplate missing) give any clue to what train this is, so it must be put down as an unrecorded product of peak period traffic pressure. (J.H.W. Kent)

106) The train behind BR Class 5 4-6-0 No 73118, from 70A Nine Elms and later named *King Leodegrance* and SR *Schools* Class 4-4-0 No 30903 *Charterhouse,* also a Nine Elms engine, could be described as '10 bogies and counting' as it stretched away round the corner to Holes Bay Junction, the heavy loading being due to the day of the week and the time of the year: Saturday 18th July 1959. (J.H.W. Kent)

107) We take our leave of Holes Bay Junction and its connection to Bath with this photograph, once again taken on 18th July 1959. SPL 20 pasted on the headcode disc of SR Unrebuilt *Battle of Britain* Class 4-6-2 No 34049 *Anti-Aircraft Command* (72B Salisbury) and the LMS carriage, make it almost certain that this is a holiday extra as it approached the junction bathed in summer sunshine. (J.H.W. Kent)

108) On the right of this picture is the transhipment shed at Furzebrook, where china clay from Pike Brothers' Isle of Purbeck tramway was loaded onto standard gauge wagons, which a work-stained SR Q Class 0-6-0 No 30541 is shunting in September 1955. The open country beyond the train is now the Wych Farm oil terminal. No 30541, a 71B Bournemouth locomotive was transferred to 70C Guildford in March 1963. (A.E. Bennett)

109) The Swanage branch train on 7th September 1955 is a mixture of old and new. SR M7 Class 0-4-4T No 30105 (71B Bournemouth) dated from 1905, about the same time as the two leading carriages. Bringing up the rear as they approach Wareham are two Bulleid coaches, forty years younger. Despite the stained appearance of No 30105 it was to remain at 71B until the end in May 1963. (A.E. Bennett)

110) The starting signals, the box from which they are worked and the trespass notice, are all LSWR at Swanage on 7th September 1955. U Class 2-6-0 No 31806, from 70D Basingstoke, is however a Southern Railway creation, entering service as *River* Class 2-6-4T No A806 *River Torridge* in 1926 and being rebuilt to the form seen here after the Sevenoaks disaster to a sister 2-6-4T. (A.E. Bennett)

111) Both of the Bincombe tunnels, situated between Monkton & Came Halt and Upwey Wishing Well Halt (what magical names) appear in this picture of SR Unrebuilt *Battle of Britain* Class 4-6-2 No 34064 *Fighter Command* (70A Nine Elms) as it coasts down the bank towards Weymouth, almost at the end of its 140 plus miles journey from Waterloo in 1957. No 34064 was fitted with a giesl oblong ejector in May 1962. (G.W. Sharpe)

112) Weymouth station has been rebuilt since these temporary canopies sheltered enthusiasts leaving the 'Greyhound' Special No 101, organised by the Railway Correspondence and Travel Society, from Waterloo to Weymouth via Yeovil on 14th August 1960. Appropriately SR T9 Class 4-4-0 No 30718 (72A Exmouth Junction) suitably polished for the occasion, is in charge of the train. (Peter Hay)

113) On 16th November 1960, SR Rebuilt *Merchant Navy* Class 4-6-2 No 35012 *United States Lines,* a longstanding inmate of 70A Nine Elms, brought invited guests to Weymouth by an all-Pullman special for a publicity cruise in the then new Channel Islands steamer *S.S. Caesarea.* Here the train has stopped for *United States Lines* to be detached, before continuing with the final leg behind a lighter engine. (C.H. Attwell)

114) After *United States Lines* had been despatched to Weymouth shed for servicing, a member of the GWR 1366 Class 0-6-0 Pannier Tanks, No 1367, a local engine, was provided for the next move of the Pullman train over the Quay Tramway to the steamer berth. The leading Pullman is *Juno,* built in 1927. No 1367 was withdrawn in October 1964 and cut up at Barry Docks in March 1965, a long time before the preservationists came along. (C.H. Attwell)

115) Another photograph of 1366 Class 0-6-0PT No 1367, this time in tandem with a fellow member of the class as they eased their way between the traffic along the Quay Tramway at Weymouth with the stock of a Channel Islands boat train in 1962. Both engines were equipped with bells to ring during their journey along the road. No 1367, along with Nos 1368 and 1369 were transferred to 72F Wadebridge in August 1962. (C.H. Attwell)

116) A packed, if smoky view of the shed yard at Weymouth in June 1961. From right to left are: BR Class 5 4-6-0 No 73018, with a sister engine behind. BR Class 9F 2-10-0 No 92208 (81C Southall), two SR Rebuilt *Merchant Navy* Class 4-6-2's Nos 35014 *Nederland Line* and 35030 *Elder Dempster Lines,* both from 70A Nine Elms, with unidentified members of the *Battle of Britain* and *Lord Nelson* Classes also visible, plus a SR N Class 2-6-0. (C.H. Attwell)

117) The little halt at Melcombe Regis was almost within shouting distance from Weymouth station but on the joint GWR/SR line to Portland and Easton. On 21st May 1951 the branch train comprised SR 02 Class 0-4-4T No 30177 and coaches from an SECR steam rail motor. Once owned by the Weymouth and Portland Joint Railway, Melcombe Regis disappeared into history when closure came in 1952. (D.K. Jones)

118) A jumble of broken masonry behind the water tower marks the site of the little engine shed at Easton, terminus of the Isle of Portland branch from Weymouth. Passenger services had ceased in 1952, eight years before the visit of this railtour behind GWR 5700 Class 0-6-0 Pannier Tank No 3737, on 14th August 1960. On its return journey to Weymouth the train was stopped by police searching for escapees from Portland Prison. (Peter Hay)

119)   The staff at Lyme Regis took a relaxed attitude when photographers strayed onto the running line appreciating that it was the only way they could record their station and its distinctive locomotives. SR 0415 Class 4-4-2T No 30583 simmered gently in the platform on 2nd July 1959. The goods shed and signalbox help to complete this fine picture. (N.L. Browne)

120)   In 1957 this scene at Lyme Regis was so long established that change seemed impossible. Yet within four years the 0415 Class 4-4-2 Tanks were no longer working the branch and within eight years there was no branch to work. No 30584 is in the foreground whilst in the left background is the diminutive engine shed which was the second on the site, the original being burnt to the ground in 1912. (Peter Hay)

CHAPTER FIVE — DEVON

121)   Moving from Dorset to Devon, once we leave Exeter behind the scene will change to one of former Great Western dominance. The DEVON chapter photograph shows an ATC shoe about to engage the warning ramp between the rails as GWR *Hall* Class 4-6-0 No 4919 *Donnington Hall* (81A Old Oak Common) sweeps over Bittaford viaduct, between Newton Abbot and Plymouth, with an up express on 19th August 1957. (Peter Hay)

122) The Southern Railway tradition of destination boards on branch line carriages was still faithfully observed on the Lyme Regis branch on 29th August 1955. 0415 Class 4-4-2T No 30582 stands ready for departure from Axminster, though how many first class passengers would join the train is doubtful. No 30582, along with two sister engines were all based at 72A Exmouth Junction being seconded to Lyme Regis shed. (N.L. Browne)

123) Out of sight in the right of the picture Combpyne's island platform accommodated only a camping coach, keeping the sun off the photographer's lens. Behind 0415 Class 4-4-2T No 30582 we observe an LSWR quarter mile post by the engine's bufferbeam and water for the station brought in churns from Lyme Regis being unloaded. By July 1961 all three members of the 0415 Class were withdrawn, with No 30583 being preserved for posterity. (A.C. Ingram)

124) Pre-cast concrete from Exmouth Junction forms the station at Colyford, closed in 1966. On 11th August 1959 the branch train from Seaton to Seaton Junction is worked by a 72A Exmouth Junction based SR M7 Class 0-4-4T No 30045 which is twinned with a pair of early Southern Region carriages. The white headcode disc highlights how filthy the locomotive was. (Peter Hay)

125) In a quiet way the Southern Region once operated quite a lavish service of local trains to the east of Exeter. At Tipton St. Johns on 4th May 1957, the two carriages behind BR Class 3 2-6-2T No 82019 from 72A Exmouth Junction, are bound for Exeter via Sidmouth Junction (now Feniton), while a train for Exmouth departs in the distance. No 82019 was drafted away to 70A Nine Elms in October 1962. (A.E. Bennett)

126)   The 1 in 37 gradient from the GWR St. Davids station at Exeter to the SR Central station caused most trains to use rear end banking assistance. On 13th October 1962, SR Unrebuilt *West Country* Class 4-6-2 No 34020 *Seaton,* a locally based Pacific from 72A Exmouth Junction, brings an express up the bank, passing one of the SR Z Class 0-8-0T bankers waiting for its next duty. (A.E. Bennett)

127)   There is plenty of steam and smoke to add to the low cloud and rain on a murky 11th April 1959 as SR E1/R Class 0-6-2T No 32697 banks a Southern Region train out of the Western Region St. Davids station at Exeter and up the 1 in 37. Part of the shed at St. Davids can be observed in the right of the picture. No 32697 was withdrawn from Exmouth Junction shed seven months after this picture was taken. (A.E. Bennett)

128) An early post-nationalisation picture of SR *King Arthur* Class 4-6-0 No 30448 *Sir Tristram* at 72A Exmouth Junction in June 1949. The engine is in the lined malachite green livery and paired with a Drummond 'water-cart' tender, eight-wheeled with all the bearings on the inside. *Sir Tristram* was to soldier on in revenue earning service until condemned from 72B Salisbury in August 1960. (G.W. Sharpe)

129) Sadly in need of being cleaned after the firebox and smokebox had been emptied, GWR 4300 Class 2-6-0 No 7311 is in the yard of its home shed at 83C Exeter (St. Davids) on 12th July 1958. Alongside No 7311 is an 85A Worcester based GWR *Castle* Class 4-6-0 No 5083 *Bath Abbey* which was destined for premature withdrawal in January 1959, being cut up at Swindon Works. (A. Swain)

130)   Looking up the Exe estuary from the heights of Langstone Rock, on 19th August 1959, Dawlish Warren station is just visible in the distance. The train behind GWR 6100 Class 2-6-2T No 6166, from 83A Newton Abbot, is a very mixed collection, with an LNER bogie leading and SR stock. Only a small number of the 6100 series served at depots in Devon. (Peter Hay)

131)   Whilst still on Langstone Rock the photographer takes advantage of the situation by panning his camera to the left where he captures another 2-6-2T on a local working on 19th August 1959. Dawlish station is in the distance to the left in this view of 5100 Class No 5164, another Newton Abbot loco, on an up train. No 5164 was despatched to 86G Pontypool Road in October 1961. (Peter Hay)

132) GWR *Grange* Class 4-6-0 No 6874 *Haughton Grange* (83B Taunton) snakes its way round the sea wall near Teignmouth in August 1959 with a westbound passenger train. In view of the mountainous inclines ahead on the main line, let us hope that this ten coach train was bound for the easier grades of the Kingswear branch. The final base for this engine was at 81F Oxford until its demise in September 1965. (H.H. Bleads)

133) A number of LMS Stanier Class 8F 2-8-0's were based at depots on the Western Region and one of their number is a long way from its home shed at 82B St. Philip's Marsh in 1958. No 48420 is heading west between the South Devon cliffs and the summer sea, near Teignmouth with a mixed freight train. 48420 was taken out of service from 87F Llanelly in April 1964. (G.W. Sharpe)

134) Only the early birds were privileged to see the passage through Dawlish of GWR *Castle* Class 4-6-0 No 5055 *Earl of Eldon* (83A Newton Abbot) hauling the 7.15 am Penzance to Paddington express, train reporting number 949. The milepost tells us that there are still 206 and a quarter miles to go but that was measured via the original route through Bristol. Paddington was just 186 miles away. (Peter Hay)

135) Early on a Saturday morning in August 1959, GWR *King* Class 4-6-0 No 6003 *King George IV,* from 81A Old Oak Common, equipped with a double chimney, rumbles over the bridge at the west end of Dawlish station with a down express, reporting number 440. *King George IV* ended its working life on the Cardiff - Paddington route, being based at Canton shed until June 1962. (Peter Hay)

136) A panoramic view of Newton Abbot on 18th August 1959 with the local shed in the background, where the outline of an unrebuilt Bulleid Pacific can be seen, GWR *Manor* Class 4-6-0 No 7808 *Cookham Manor,* a local engine, sets out on a local passenger working to Kingswear. Happily, after withdrawal from 85B Gloucester (Horton Road) in December 1965, *Cookham Manor* was preserved. (Peter Hay)

137) Engines can no longer be turned at Kingswear though steam is still to be seen there. In 1957 GWR 4300 Class 2-6-0 No 7316, from 83C Exeter (St. Davids) had worked in with a stopping train and it was certainly not going to return to Newton Abbot tender-first. No 7316, a longstanding occupant at Exeter St. Davids, succumbed to the inevitable withdrawal in September 1962. (N.E. Preedy)

138) Newton Abbot has been left behind us, as has Aller Junction and the Torbay branch, as GWR *County* Class 4-6-0 No 1014 *County of Glamorgan,* from 82A Bristol (Bath Road) sweeps round the curve on the approach to Dainton bank with a lightweight Liverpool - Plymouth express consisting of seven coaches on 29th May 1959. *County of Glamorgan* had been modified with a double chimney in November 1956. (J. Head)

139) Cattle trucks and milk tanks seem to comprise most of the load that GWR *Hall* Class 4-6-0 No 4975 *Umberslade Hall* (83A Newton Abbot), seen here in superb external condition, is dragging up the 1 in 36 near the summit of Dainton bank. Despite having steam to spare its progress would have been almost impossible in April 1960 without rear end assistance from a 2-6-2T. (B.W.L. Brooksbank)

140) This iron footbridge across the line at Totnes was removed in 1988 after an argument with a crane. On 19th August 1959 it still allowed intending passengers to make a last minute dash to catch this up train, headed by a more than work-stained GWR *Castle* Class 4-6-0 No 5029 *Nunney Castle,* shedded at nearby 83A Newton Abbot. Withdrawn in December 1963, *Nunney Castle* is preserved at GWS Didcot. (Peter Hay)

141) GWR *King* Class 4-6-0 No 6004 *King George III,* from 83D Laira (Plymouth) has steam to spare on Rattery bank with the down *Cornish Riviera Express* on 10th July 1955, perhaps due to the efforts of the fireman of the pilot engine BR Class 4 4-6-0 No 75007, which was far from its home base at 86C Cardiff (Canton). Note that the fireman of No 6004 was taking things easy. (J. Head)

142) GWR *Castle* Class 4-6-0 No 7014 *Caerhays Castle,* an 82A Bristol (Bath Road) engine fitted with a double chimney, is assisted by an unidentified sister locomotive, a single chimney version, as it swings through the curve at the eastern end of Brent station, after the 1 in 50 climb up Rattery bank from Totnes in the summer of 1959. On the right the single line Kingsbridge branch comes in from the south. (Peter Hay)

143) No longer can we change at Brent for all stations to Kingsbridge and on 16th August 1959 neither could passengers on the up *Cornishman,* the 10.35 am Penzance to Wolverhampton. It speeds through the sun-soaked station behind GWR *Castle* Class 4-6-0 No 7022 *Hereford Castle,* from 83D Laira (Plymouth), which had been equipped with a double chimney in December 1957 and was to survive in service until June 1965. (Peter Hay)

144)   An idyllic scene in the summer of 1959. Properly uniformed with cap and polished shoes, the porter at Gara Bridge station looks on as the two coach Kingsbridge branch train arrives behind a bunker-first GWR 4500 Class 2-6-2T No 5558, from 83A Newton Abbot. Though the vegetation is lush the station is immaculate and the compact signalbox and lower quadrant signal help to complete the picture. (Peter Hay)

145)   The branch to Kingsbridge closed in 1963 but four years earlier on 19th August 1959 the smartly maintained terminus was the scene of activity proper for a holiday resort in the summer months. The branch train, headed by GWR 4500 Class 2-6-2T No 5558, stands ready to connect with the main line at Brent. There is a spare set of carriages in the siding and in the bay stands a van with doors open for the 'luggage in advance'. (Peter Hay)

146) Summer Saturdays in 1959 produced many additional trains for holidaymakers, like this one on 19th August, behind GWR *Castle* Class 4-6-0 No 5075 *Wellington,* allocated to 83C Exeter (St. Davids). It is just entering Wrangaton at the summit of the climb from Totnes. The water crane was mainly used by goods trains as only local services called here. The station closed during 1959. (Peter Hay)

147) The consequences for a heavy eastbound train suffering from a signal stop on the 1 in 42 of Hemerdon bank, are all too obvious in this picture. Steam envelopes both GWR *Hall* Class 4-6-0 No 6941 *Fillongley Hall* (83D Laira — Plymouth) and an unidentified GWR *King* Class 4-6-0 as they struggle to restart the train, heavily loaded in the holiday month of August 1958. Note the chalked reporting number 565. (G.W. Sharpe)

148)   GWR *Castle* Class 4-6-0 No 4098 *Kidwelly Castle* (83A Newton Abbot), has only a light 8-coach train as it passes Cornwood signalbox on 19th August 1959, with an up train, all in the BR red livery. The fireman is so much on top of his work that he can afford to relax and hang a leg out of the cab doorway. Like Wrangaton, Cornwood station also closed during 1959. (Peter Hay)

149)   Bittaford Platform, between Wrangaton and Ivybridge (another to suffer the cuts of 1959) was the official name of this modest erection on the main line to Plymouth. When GWR *Hall* Class 4-6-0 No 6941 *Fillongley Hall* raced through with a down train on 19th August 1959, Bittaford had already been closed for five months. *Fillongley Hall* fared better than the station, surviving another five years. (Peter Hay)

150) Steam has been shut off on GWR *Castle* Class 4-6-0 No 7031 *Cromwells Castle,* an 83D Laira (Plymouth) engine, as it gallops through Plympton at the foot of Hemerdon bank on 19th August 1959. The leading vehicle is a Royal Mail tender, returning westwards for the evening's up mail. Withdrawn from 85A Worcester in July 1963, *Cromwells Castle* languished in store there until cut up in June 1964. (Peter Hay)

151) We finish this chapter with a rare print of Plymouth (Friary) station. This quiet SR terminus sprang to life occasionally, as when SR Unrebuilt *Battle of Britain* Class 4-6-2 No 34109 *Sir Trafford Leigh-Mallory* left for Waterloo on 20th August 1958. The unidentified GWR 4300 Class 2-6-0 on the right has a similar headcode, but it wouldn't be going all the way to London. (A.E. Bennett)

CHAPTER SIX — CORNWALL

152) Trains between Liskeard and Looe still reverse at Coombe Junction. GWR 4500 Class 2-6-2T No 4565 (83E St. Blazey) has just run round its train before taking the circuitous climb to the main line at Liskeard station, three quarters of a mile to the right of Moorswater viaduct in the background. In August 1959 only the stub of the 1844 line under the viaduct and up to Caradon mines remained. (Peter Hay)

153)   Saltash station is immediately west of the Royal Albert bridge by which the railway enters Cornwall and on 18th August 1959 was the terminus for the intensive service of local Plymouth trains. GWR 6400 Class 0-6-0PT No 6419, a Laira engine, is fitted, like the rest of the class, for push and pull working and is seen taking water before crossing over to the up line for the return trip to Plymouth. (Peter Hay)

154)   83F Truro based GWR *Grange* Class 4-6-0 No 6828 *Trellech Grange,* restarts a heavy eastbound holiday express from Menheniot, between Liskeard and St. Germans on 18th August 1959. Made surplus to Cornish requirements in September 1961, *Trellech Grange* was despatched to less pleasant surroundings at 84B Oxley (Wolverhampton) from where it was withdrawn in July 1963. (Peter Hay)

155) Is the porter with the barrow expecting parcels, or passengers with luggage from the Looe train as it stops at Liskeard station? The branch platform here is at right angles to the main line ones behind the camera, a consequence of the complex history of the area. The branch line engine on 18th August 1959 is GWR 4500 Class 2-6-2T No 4559, from 83E St. Blazey, withdrawn in October 1960. (Peter Hay)

156) This is the site of Moorswater Junction where the long defunct Liskeard & Caradon Railway made an end-on connection with the Liskeard & Looe line. Coombe Junction, where the connection from Liskeard on the main line is made, lies beyond Moorswater viaduct on which an unidentified GWR *Hall* Class 4-6-0 heads the 1.30 pm Paddington - Penzance which, in August 1959, was named *The Royal Duchy*. (Peter Hay)

157)	Relaying with concrete sleepers seemed to be planned in August 1959 as GWR 4500 Class 2-6-2T No 4565, from 83E St. Blazey, brought its two coach train to a halt to collect two passengers from St. Keyne (for St. Keyne's Well) on the Looe branch. There are oil lamps to light the modest platform and 'bus shelter' after dark. Withdrawn from St. Blazey in October 1961, No 4565 was scrapped in March 1962. (Peter Hay)

158)	Another photograph of GWR 4500 Class 2-6-2T No 4559, which worked the Looe branch on 18th August 1959, here arriving at the terminus beside the tranquil river. Steam has long since been replaced by diesel traction, so the water tank on its stone tower no longer feeds thirsty branch engines. Today, a 'basic railway' concrete erection serves Looe passengers. (Peter Hay)

159) The fact that the line into the goods shed on the left is on the level gives some idea of the drag on GWR *Hall* Class 4-6-0 No 4928 *Gatacre Hall,* from 83D Laira (Plymouth), as it pounded up the curving incline through Bodmin Road, with an eastbound freight working on 17th August 1959. The gradient is at 1 in 74. *Gatacre Hall* survived in active service until December 1963, from 87B Duffryn Yard. (Peter Hay)

160) GWR driving auto trailer No. W252W leads No W455W and GWR 4500 Class 2-6-2T No 5572, another engine from the Laira allocation, as the Fowey branch train arrives at Lostwithiel on 17th August 1959. The next movement through the station was the thunderous passage of the up *Cornish Riviera Express,* behind a gleaming GWR *Castle* Class 4-6-0. No 5572 is preserved at Didcot. (Peter Hay)

161)   On the 1 in 36 single track (direct line) between Fowey and Par, GWR 5700 Class 0-6-0PT No 9655 struggles along with
        a train of empties on their way back to the china clay workings north of St. Austell, on 17th August 1959. Since 1968, this
        line has been a road used by lorries which now carry the traffic. No 9655, a longstanding inhabitant of 83E St. Blazey, was
        transferred to 86G Pontypool Road in April 1962. (Peter Hay)

162)   The evening sun lights up a grubby GWR *Grange* Class 4-6-0 No 6826 *Nannerth Grange,* from 83G Penzance, as it skirts
        the shore of the harbour at Par, with a smart BR set on a down stopping train on 16th August 1959. Before withdrawal in
        May 1965, *Nannerth Grange* was to work from 83D Laira (Plymouth), 81D Reading and finally 88A Cardiff East Dock. Birds,
        Morriston disposed of the locomotive in July 1965. (Peter Hay)

163) The 7.00 pm Newquay to Plymouth passenger approaches the connection from the closed station at St. Blazey to the main line at Par, on 17th August 1959, behind GWR *Hall* Class 4-6-0 No 4930 *Hagley Hall* (83B Taunton). This piece of line has a curious history, being built by Squire Treffry as a private mineral railway parallel to the overgrown canal below the train, opened in 1842. (Peter Hay)

164) On 16th August 1959, GWR *County* Class 4-6-0 No 1002 *County of Berks* was based at 83G Penzance and it is seen entering St. Austell station with a short train of milk tanks. In 1959 the scene was still Great Western in nearly every detail. *County of Berks* ended its working life at Shrewsbury shed in September 1963 being scrapped far from its birthplace of Swindon, at Wards, Broughton Lane, Sheffield. (Peter Hay)

165) Grampound Road situated between St. Austell and Truro, closed like so many wayside stations in 1964, but on 16th August 1959 trains still called there, like this local working from Plymouth. Coming up a gradient of 1 in 83 the driver of GWR 4500 Class 2-6-2T No 4585 (83E St. Blazey) is unable to shut off steam until well into the platform. (Peter Hay)

166)　It is 10.52 am, under threatening skies and the up *Cornish Riveria Express* is pulling out of Truro on 12th August 1960 behind GWR *Castle* Class 4-6-0 No 5066 *Sir Felix Pole,* from 81A Old Oak Common, dead on time and with a spotless rake of BR Mk I stock. No 5066 was named *Wardour Castle* until 1956 and fitted with a double chimney in April 1959. It was withdrawn from Old Oak in September 1962. (Peter Hay)

167)　Scorrier, between Truro and Redruth, was another casualty of the 1964 closure programme, five years after GWR *Grange* Class 4-6-0 No 6849 *Walton Grange,* an 83G Penzance engine, passed by on 14th August 1959, with a load of holidaymakers bound for the delights of West Cornwall. *Walton Grange* was condemned from 81F Oxford, in December 1965, almost at the end of steam on the Western Region. (Peter Hay)

168)   A level crossing spanning both the main line and the Helston branch tracks required extra long gates at Gwinear Road, between St. Erth and Redruth, where GWR *County* Class 4-6-0 No 1007 *County of Brecknock* has paused with an up train in August 1959. The up main signals are fitted to the footbridge because of the sharp curve, and the GWR 4500 Class 2-6-2T on the Helston service peeps out from behind the signalbox. (Peter Hay)

169)   Short trousers and long socks pre-date the now universal jeans and indicate the 1950's as the time when these boys had a holiday at Helston. GWR 4500 Class 2-6-2T No 4570, from 83G Penzance, is the engine being closely inspected on 13th August 1959. No 4570 was re-allocated to 83D Laira in July 1962, withdrawn in January 1963 and cut up at Cashmores, Newport in August 1964. (Peter Hay)

170) Holiday traffic started early on summer Saturdays in the 1950's, so the morning shadows are still long on 14th August 1956 as GWR *Hall* Class 4-6-0 No 4905 *Barton Hall* (83A Newton Abbot) slows to call at Hayle. On the right is the commencement of the branch down to Hayle Harbour. Note the placing of bull-head rails on their sides as a safety device outside the down line rail over the viaduct. (Peter Hay)

171) GWR *Hall* Class 4-6-0 No 6931 *Aldborough Hall,* from 83E St. Blazey, nears the end of its journey westwards to Penzance as it passes through the lush Cornish countryside with a down express, near St. Erth on a hot 14th August 1959. *Aldborough Hall* was another member of the class that ended its working life at 81F Oxford, this time in October 1965, being scrapped at Birds, Risca in February 1966. (Peter Hay)

172) The signalman at St. Erth, having collected the St. Ives branch token from the fireman of GWR 4500 Class 2-6-2T No 4571 (83G Penzance) makes for the signalbox on the right. Compare the two stop signals: the one on the left is on a tubular metal post while the one on the right was still of timber in 1959. The tracks in the foreground lead to Plymouth and Paddington. (Peter Hay)

173) We can still change, as the sign says, at St. Erth for St. Ives, but we cannot ride behind GWR *Grange* Class 4-6-0's like No 6849 *Walton Grange* because none of them have been preserved. Introduced in 1936 they were all withdrawn from service by the end of 1965. On 14th August 1959 there are plenty of trolleys but no passengers to watch this up train make its early evening call. (Peter Hay)

174) On weekdays the 8.00 am local passenger from St. Erth to St. Ives was a mixed train, seen here running beside the mudflats of the Hayle estuary behind GWR 4500 Class 2-6-2T No 4566, based at 83G Penzance. St. Erth's distant signal is behind the brake van which brings up the rear of the train on 9th August 1959. Withdrawn in April 1962, No 4566 is now actively preserved on the Severn Valley Railway. (Peter Hay)

175) A fine photograph of the rural setting of St. Ives, on 14th August 1959. Note the loading gauge and catch-points in the foreground. For many years this branch was worked almost exclusively by GWR 4500 Class 2-6-2 Tanks, amongst them No 4571 with an 83A Newton Abbot shedplate. Beyond the five coach train, to the right of the photograph is St. Ives station. The end for No 4571 came in March 1961. (Peter Hay)

176)   Another shot of GWR 4500 Class 2-6-2T No 4571 taken on the same day in 1959. The sunlit waters of St. Ives Bay and the Hayle sand-dunes form a background for No 4571 and its five coach train. They are braking for a stop at Carbis Bay station, the last call before St. Ives. After condemnation from Penzance shed in March 1961, No 4571 was cut up at Swindon Works in April 1961. (Peter Hay)

177)   Marazion was the last station before Penzance until its closure in 1964, and it was quite bare of intending passengers as GWR *Hall* Class 4-6-0 No 4928 *Gatacre Hall,* from 83D Laira (Plymouth) passed through with a down local freight on 13th August 1959. Before withdrawal from 87B Duffryn Yard, in December 1963, *Gatacre Hall* also served from 86C Cardiff (Canton) and 87F Llanelly. (Peter Hay)

178)   We end our sojourn along the South Coast, with two photographs taken at 83G Penzance, on 24th September 1963, twelve
months after it had lost its official steam allocation. A visitor to the shed on this day is GWR *Castle* Class 4-6-0 No 7022
Hereford Castle, from 83D Laira (Plymouth), in steam in the yard. Although it had been given the 'whitewash treatment' there
was a general air of neglect about it. (Peter Hay)

179)   The fires had been drawn on these GWR 4500 Class 2-6-2 Tanks, some twelve months before this picture was taken. Bereft
of number and shedplates, Nos 5537 and 5562 stand in the weeds at the side of the shed, awaiting their last journey to the
breakers yard at Cashmores Newport. No 5562 was cut up in March 1964 but No 5537 lingered on until November of that
year after a period of further storage at Laira. (Peter Hay)